HUMAN ANATOMY
activity book
FOR KIDS

HUMAN ANATOMY
activity book
FOR KIDS
HANDS-ON LEARNING
FOR GRADES 4–7

SHANNAN MUSKOPF, MS

Illustrations by Christy Ni

ROCKRIDGE
PRESS

To my niece, Annabell,
a curious girl who is growing up near the same lake I did.
May she find many fascinating things in those woods.

Interior and Cover Designer: Angie Chiu
Art Producer: Tom Hood
Editor: Annie Choi
Production Editor: Mia Moran
Illustrations © Christy Ni 2020

ISBN: Print 978-1-64876-016-7 | eBook 978-1-64876-017-4
R0

CONTENTS

INTRODUCTION

Humans have always been curious about their bodies. We wonder how they work, what makes us sick, and how to fix things when something goes wrong.

From a very young age, I was curious about the body and fascinated by many of the things other kids found "gross." I grew up near a lake, and my first laboratory was in the woods nearby. It was a place where I could find all kinds of creatures and plants. I would sometimes find bleached skulls and try to guess what animals they belonged to. I figured out that many were raccoons, opossums, or even squirrels! I wrote this book for curious kids like you who love exploring and learning about the inner workings of your own bodies.

When I went to college, I learned the art of dissection. This is the process of carefully cutting apart an animal to learn about its body and how it works. I even worked on cadavers, which are dead humans. I saw what we look like on the inside and discovered that it wasn't nearly as shocking or gross as I had imagined.

We are all put together the same way—sometimes with small differences—a stomach in the center, the heart above it, and long blood vessels that stretch from head to toe. I was delighted to find that if I pulled certain tendons in the arm, the fingers would move. I learned that you can diagnose sickness by looking closely at organs. I loved learning about the body!

People probably ask you all the time, "What do you want to be when you grow up?" Here's a secret that adults won't tell you: Most of us didn't know what we wanted to be. Many of us still didn't know when we got older. Our paths often change as we grow. I discovered that I had a lot more passion for learning about the body than for fixing it. As you read this book, you may find that you have a passion for learning all about the lungs, fixing broken bones, or curing cancer—figure out what you find most interesting and keep exploring.

I eventually became a science teacher, and now I teach kids like you about the human body. My classroom is filled with skulls, models, and even jars with dead things inside that are good resources for my students. You won't find jars or skulls on these pages, but you will learn all kinds of amazing things you didn't know about the body. I hope you love learning about it as much as I did.

Throughout this book, you will find activity pages to reinforce things you've learned. When you are ready to experiment, check out the "Try This at Home" activities for some fun hands-on ways to discover more about the body. Finally, I hope that if you ever find a skull in the woods, you stop and take a closer look!

Let's get started!

YOUR AMAZING BODY

The human body comes in all shapes and sizes. But underneath it all, our organs are the same, and they work together to keep us alive. The body's amazing ability to adapt has allowed humans to spread across the entire planet and live in some of the most difficult environments. People can live in areas that are very cold or very hot and even places like high mountains, where the air is so thin it's difficult to breathe!

The tallest human being who ever lived was Robert Wadlow, known as the "Alton Giant," who was 8 feet, 11 inches tall.

The record for shortest human goes to Chandra Bahadur Dangi, who was only 21.5 inches tall.

DID YOU KNOW?

Anatomy is the study of the parts of the body, like the heart and lungs. **Physiology** focuses on how those parts work. Each body system is made up of **organs** that work together to perform important functions. All the body systems depend on one another to keep you healthy.

Your organs must keep the conditions inside your body consistent—even when the outside environment changes. When you get hot, your body sweats to cool off. When you are cold, your body shivers to keep warm. This state of balance inside the body is called **homeostasis**. If you cannot maintain this state of balance, you could get sick or even die.

NERVOUS SYSTEM
receives and sends information to the body and controls everything from breathing to sweating

It can take up to 14 years of study after high school to become a fully licensed doctor.

LYMPHATIC SYSTEM
locates infections and disease in the body and eliminates them

RESPIRATORY SYSTEM
takes in oxygen and removes carbon dioxide from the body

ENDOCRINE SYSTEM
secretes chemicals called hormones to control growth and development

CARDIOVASCULAR SYSTEM
moves blood through the body so it can deliver oxygen and nutrients to cells

DIGESTIVE SYSTEM
breaks down food into nutrients the body can use

REPRODUCTIVE SYSTEM
produces cells needed to create a new human and a place for it to grow

URINARY SYSTEM
removes waste from the blood

SKELETAL SYSTEM
provides a protective framework for the body and produces blood cells

MUSCULAR SYSTEM
makes the body move

In the 18th century, medical schools needed bodies to work on so doctors could learn how to treat patients. Criminals, called resurrectionists, would raid cemeteries at night and sell bodies to the schools.

YOUR BODY'S BUILDING BLOCKS

Every organ in your body is made of millions of single cells that are so tiny you can only see them with a microscope. Some are long and thin, while others are flat and stacked tightly together. Some cells even have tiny hairs on their surface. Cells group together to form **tissues**. Tissues group together to form organs, such as the stomach and the brain. The human body has about 200 different types of cells!

The smallest human cell is the sperm cell and the largest is the egg cell. But human eggs are still small—about the width of a strand of hair.

Nicknamed the "powerhouses of the cell," **mitochondria** provide energy for the cell. Cells that work the hardest, like muscle cells, have the most mitochondria.

DID YOU KNOW?

Each type of cell looks different because of its specific job, but all cells have many things in common.

- A cell holds watery material called **cytoplasm**.

- The cytoplasm is surrounded by a **cell membrane** that can let certain kinds of materials in and out of the cell.

- Tiny **organelles** in the cytoplasm perform different tasks. Some organelles digest the cell's food, some provide energy, and others transport substances inside the cell.

- The **nucleus** contains instructions in the form of DNA.

Each cell works like a little factory. The organelles follow instructions from the nucleus to build proteins, which help the cell do its specific job.

About 3 percent of your total body mass is bacteria. If a person weighs 100 pounds, that's 3 pounds of bacteria!

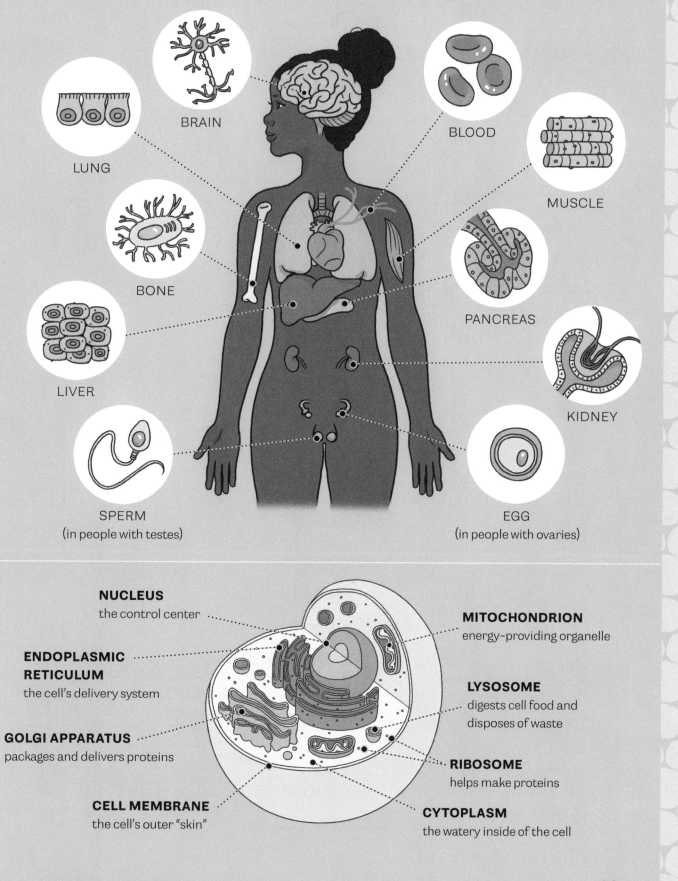

LUNG

BRAIN

BLOOD

MUSCLE

BONE

LIVER

PANCREAS

KIDNEY

SPERM
(in people with testes)

EGG
(in people with ovaries)

NUCLEUS
the control center

MITOCHONDRION
energy-providing organelle

ENDOPLASMIC RETICULUM
the cell's delivery system

LYSOSOME
digests cell food and
disposes of waste

GOLGI APPARATUS
packages and delivers proteins

RIBOSOME
helps make proteins

CELL MEMBRANE
the cell's outer "skin"

CYTOPLASM
the watery inside of the cell

YOUR BODY'S BUILDING BLOCKS

ACTIVITY: FILL IN THE BLANKS

Can you label all the parts of this cell? See page 67 for help.

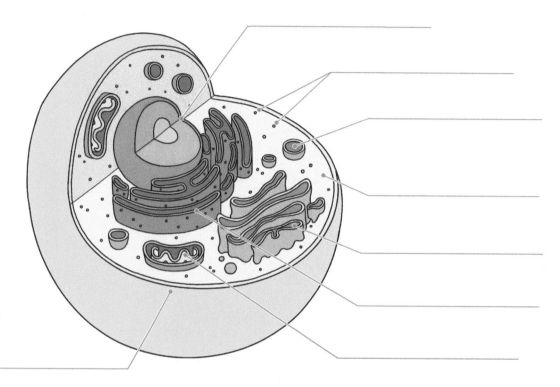

WORD BANK

nucleus   mitochondrion   cytoplasm

cell membrane   ribosome   Golgi apparatus

endoplasmic reticulum   lysosome

➡ Try This at Home

Try building your own cell! Look around your house and in the pantry. Can you find objects that look like the cell parts you just learned about? Gather materials like paper clips, toothpicks, and macaroni to build a 3D model of a cell. Using the diagram in this chapter as a guide, build your cell on cardboard and then take a "cell-fie" to show your friends.

ACTIVITY: HELP DR. MITO

Doctor Mito helps cells that are not feeling well. Read each of the following statements from his patients and help him determine what part of the cell is sick. Each symptom is based on the function of that cell part.

Cell patient symptoms	What cell part is causing the problem?
"Doctor Mito, I just can't seem to get moving in the morning. I'm so tired, I can't do anything!"	_____
"There is so much waste in my cytoplasm, I can't seem to get rid of it. It's really piling up!"	_____
"Doc, I don't know what I'm doing. I'm ready to get to work, but I don't have any instructions!"	_____
"I keep trying to order materials, but nothing is coming inside. Also, my water keeps leaking out."	_____
"Doctor, is there something you can do? I made all these beautiful proteins, but they aren't getting packaged."	_____
"The nucleus sent me perfect instructions, but when I try to build the proteins, they come out all wrong."	_____
"Doc! I was trying to move proteins to the other side of the cell, but they just won't move at all. They're stuck on one side."	_____

Answers on page 67.

A STRONG FOUNDATION

The bones in your skeletal system protect important organs, help you move, and produce blood cells. They give your body shape. Your bones also store calcium and other minerals your body needs. They come in different shapes and sizes and are connected to other bones by **ligaments** at the **joints**. You were born with about 300 bones, but over time, some bones fuse together. By the time you are an adult, you will have 206 bones in your body.

Can you crack your knuckles? When you stretch a joint, a tiny bubble of gas expands in the empty space. The bubble makes a popping sound when it returns to its original position.

Most humans have 12 pairs of ribs that protect organs, like the heart and lungs. A few people have 13 pairs. The extras are called **cervical ribs** and are found in the neck.

DID YOU KNOW?

Muscles need something to attach to. That's where bones come in.

Many muscles are attached to bones with **tendons**. To create movement, like walking, tendons pull on bones at the joints. Joints are the connecting points between bones that can bend and rotate.

Each bone has **cartilage** at both ends to protect it at the joints. Cartilage is made of a smooth stretchy material called **collagen**. It acts like a cushion between the bones. Without cartilage in your joints, your bones would grind together and you would feel pain when you move.

There are two types of bone tissue: **compact bone** and **spongy bone**. The hard outer "shell" of a bone is compact bone. The inside of most bones is filled with spongy bone. It contains **red marrow** for making blood cells. But don't be fooled by its name—spongy bone is actually very hard and strong! **Yellow marrow** stores fats. It is found in a hollow area in the center of the long leg and arm bones.

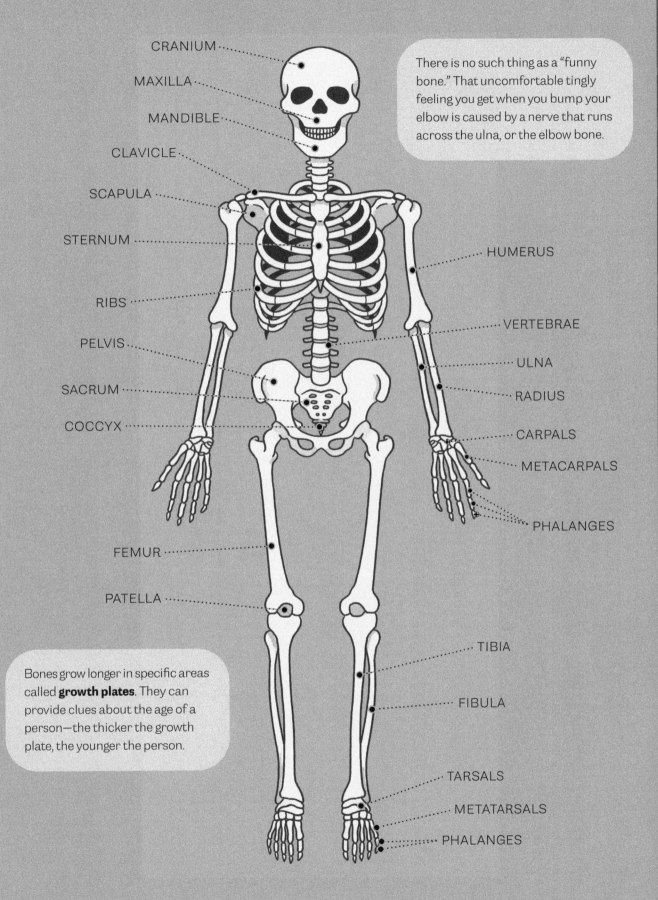

CRANIUM

MAXILLA

MANDIBLE

CLAVICLE

SCAPULA

STERNUM

RIBS

PELVIS

SACRUM

COCCYX

FEMUR

PATELLA

There is no such thing as a "funny bone." That uncomfortable tingly feeling you get when you bump your elbow is caused by a nerve that runs across the ulna, or the elbow bone.

HUMERUS

VERTEBRAE

ULNA

RADIUS

CARPALS

METACARPALS

PHALANGES

TIBIA

FIBULA

Bones grow longer in specific areas called **growth plates**. They can provide clues about the age of a person—the thicker the growth plate, the younger the person.

TARSALS

METATARSALS

PHALANGES

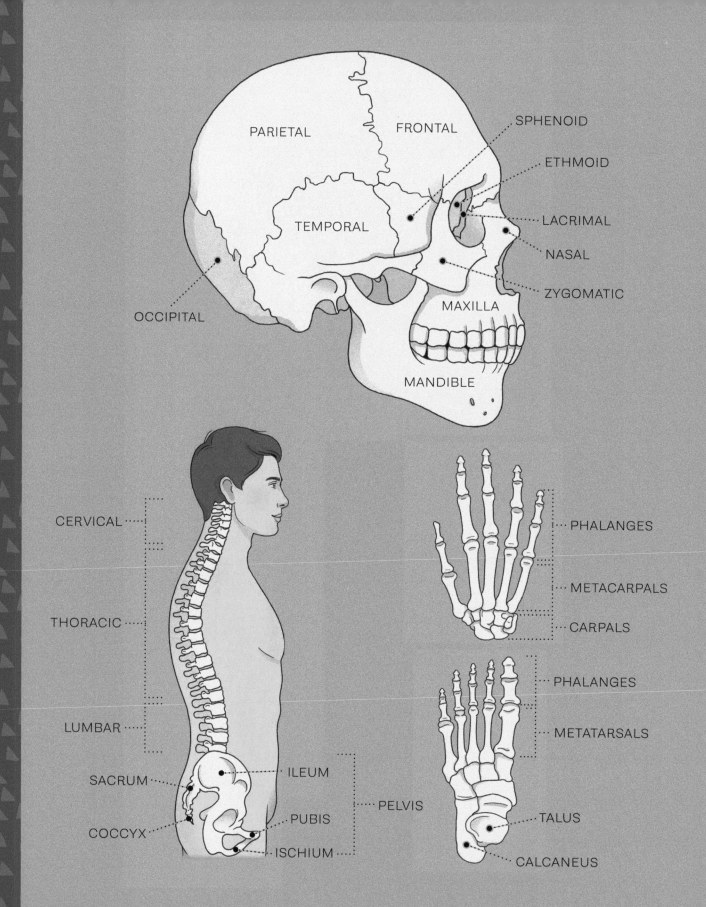

PARIETAL

FRONTAL

SPHENOID

ETHMOID

LACRIMAL

NASAL

ZYGOMATIC

TEMPORAL

MAXILLA

OCCIPITAL

MANDIBLE

CERVICAL

THORACIC

LUMBAR

SACRUM

COCCYX

ILEUM

PUBIS

ISCHIUM

PELVIS

PHALANGES

METACARPALS

CARPALS

PHALANGES

METATARSALS

TALUS

CALCANEUS

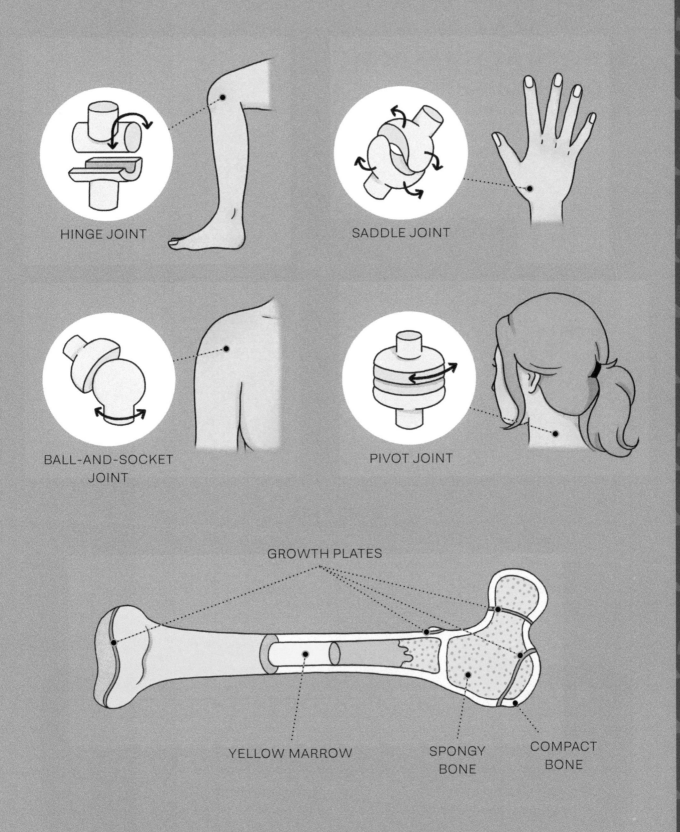

HINGE JOINT

SADDLE JOINT

BALL-AND-SOCKET
JOINT

PIVOT JOINT

GROWTH PLATES

YELLOW MARROW

SPONGY
BONE

COMPACT
BONE

ACTIVITY: NAME THE BONE!

Can you label all the bones in the skeleton?
See page 67 for help.

WORD BANK

cranium	radius	phalanges	tibia
mandible	ulna	pelvis	fibula
scapula	carpals	femur	tarsals
humerus	sternum		

➡ Try This at Home

Next time you have chicken for dinner, take a leg bone and try to bend it. What happens? It is probably too hard to bend. Try soaking the bone in a jar filled with vinegar for three days. This will remove the calcium from the bone. Calcium is what makes bones hard and strong. Bend the bone after it has soaked. How is it different than the way it felt before?

ACTIVITY: CROSSWORD PUZZLE

Use the clues provided to fill in the crossword puzzle.

Across

2. The knee is this type of joint

6. Upper arm bone

9. Kneecap

10. Bones of the wrist

12. Jawbone

Down

1. Upper leg bone

3. Shinbone

4. Bones of the spine

5. Finger bones

7. Elbow bone

8. Bones of the ankle

11. Bones that protect heart and lungs

Answers on page 67.

MUSCLE
POWER

Place your arm flat on a table and pull your hand toward your chest. When you do this, a muscle in your upper arm—called the **biceps**—contracts, or shortens. Extend your arm away from your body. You are now making a different muscle contract—your **triceps** on the back of your arm. Muscles work together like this, pulling on opposite sides of your joints to allow different types of movement.

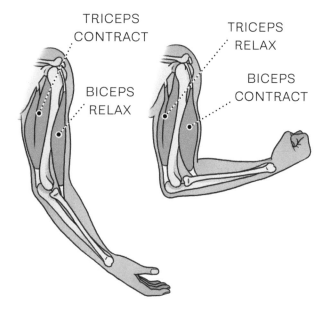

TRICEPS
CONTRACT

BICEPS
RELAX

TRICEPS
RELAX

BICEPS
CONTRACT

DID YOU KNOW?

Muscle cells contain thousands of tiny protein strings called **myofibrils**. These strings are connected to your nervous system, which lets your brain control when they contract. Myofibrils form bundles, like strings gathered into a thicker rope, that are strong enough to move your bones or lift weights.

Skeletal muscles are muscles that attach to bones and are **voluntary**. These are movements you make on purpose—like picking up a pencil or kicking a ball.

Other muscles, like the **cardiac muscles** of the heart and the **smooth muscles** of your digestive system, are **involuntary**. Your heart beats and your intestines contract to move food along without you consciously telling them to do these things.

When you move your muscles, they produce heat. In fact, most of the heat in your body comes from muscle movement. Shivering generates heat when you get cold.

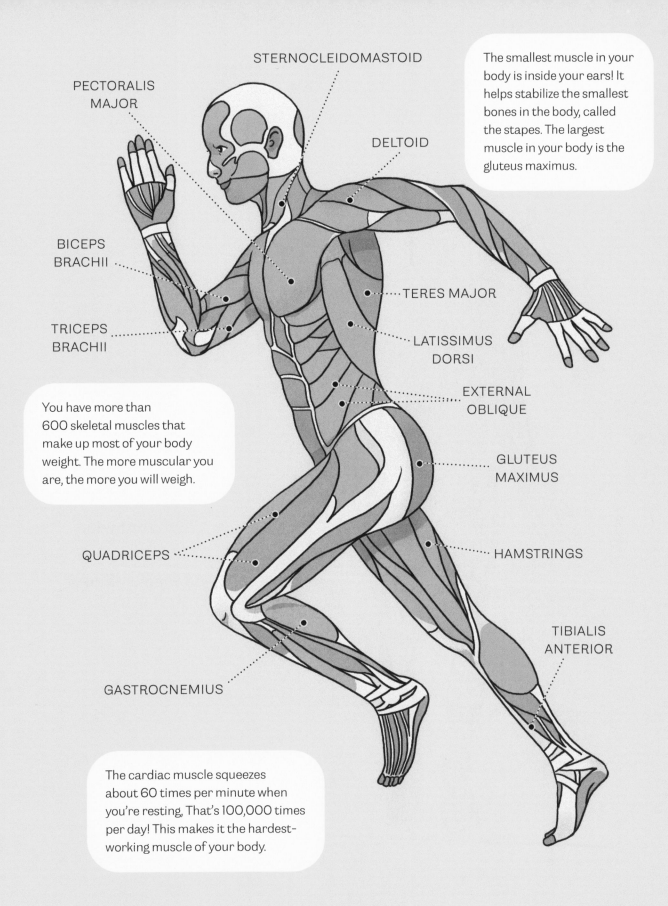

PECTORALIS
MAJOR

STERNOCLEIDOMASTOID

DELTOID

The smallest muscle in your body is inside your ears! It helps stabilize the smallest bones in the body, called the stapes. The largest muscle in your body is the gluteus maximus.

BICEPS
BRACHII

TRICEPS
BRACHII

TERES MAJOR

LATISSIMUS
DORSI

EXTERNAL
OBLIQUE

You have more than 600 skeletal muscles that make up most of your body weight. The more muscular you are, the more you will weigh.

GLUTEUS
MAXIMUS

QUADRICEPS

HAMSTRINGS

TIBIALIS
ANTERIOR

GASTROCNEMIUS

The cardiac muscle squeezes about 60 times per minute when you're resting, That's 100,000 times per day! This makes it the hardest-working muscle of your body.

MUSCLE POWER

ACTIVITY: MATCH THE MUSCLES

Draw an arrow to indicate the location of each of the following muscles on the diagram.

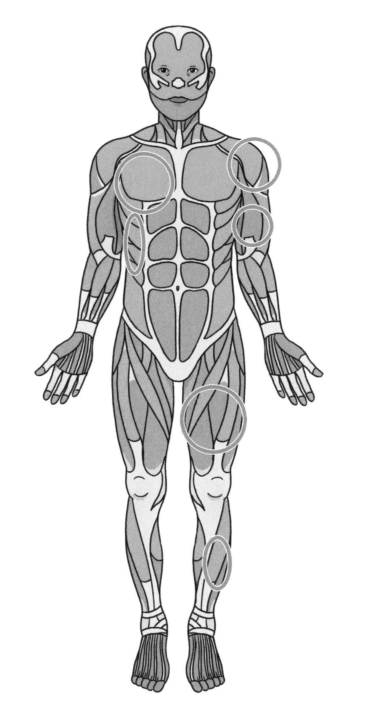

- biceps

- quadriceps

- deltoid

- pectoralis major

- tibialis anterior

- external oblique

Answers on page 68.

ACTIVITY: DO YOU KNOW YOUR MUSCLES?

Circle the correct word that completes each sentence. See page 68 for help.

1. The type of muscle found in the heart is [skeletal / cardiac / smooth].

2. The muscle that pulls your arm toward the body is the [triceps / biceps].

3. The largest muscle is the [gluteus maximus / triceps].

4. Muscles are made of strings called [neurons / myofibrils].

5. Muscle movement produces [cold / heat].

6. Skeletal muscles are [voluntary / involuntary].

7. Smooth muscles are [voluntary / involuntary].

8. The muscle that works opposite the biceps is the [gluteus / triceps].

9. The hardest-working muscle in the body is the [cardiac / gluteus].

10. Muscles that you do not consciously control are called [voluntary / involuntary].

➡ Try This at Home

Muscle fatigue occurs when you have used a muscle so much that it becomes tired and can no longer contract. Place a rubber band so it is snug around your closed fingers as shown. Now, stretch your fingers apart repeatedly. How many times you can stretch your fingers before your fingers start to feel tired? If you do this regularly, you should see an increase in the number of stretches you can do!

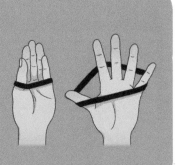

YOUR BODY'S HIGHWAY SYSTEM

The **circulatory system** is a network of heart and blood vessels that lets your blood deliver oxygen and nutrients to every part of your body. Can you spot a vein on your arm extending from your wrist to your elbow? The vein looks blue on the outside, but the blood flowing through it is red. Red blood cells contain a protein called **hemoglobin** that carries oxygen and gives blood its red color.

When you put your hand over your heart, you place it on the left side of your chest. This is where you can feel the **left ventricle**, the strongest part of the heart.

Doctors use a **sphygmomanometer** to measure blood pressure. A blood pressure reading shows how hard your blood is pushing against the walls of your blood vessels.

DID YOU KNOW?

The heart pumps blood to the lungs, where it picks up oxygen. Then the heart pumps the oxygenated blood to the rest of the body. This cycle is also called a **double-loop system** because the blood travels through the heart twice—heart to lungs, lungs to heart, then to the rest of the body.

Blood going to the body leaves the heart through a large **artery** called the **aorta**. The aorta branches into smaller arteries, and then into even smaller **capillaries** that deliver oxygen to tissues.

Blood returns to the heart through veins. The largest vein is the **vena cava**. After entering the heart, the deoxygenated blood is sent to the lungs through the **pulmonary artery**, where it picks up oxygen and starts the cycle all over again.

Humans have four **blood types**: A, B, AB, and O. When a person needs blood, like after an accident, doctors must be careful to match the blood types. Getting the wrong blood can be dangerous!

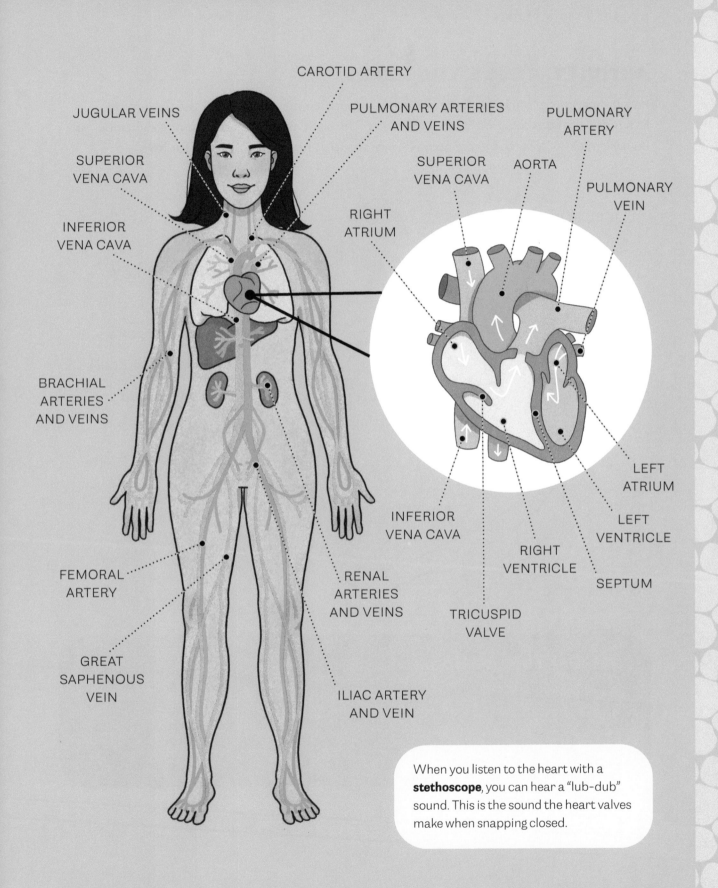

CAROTID ARTERY

JUGULAR VEINS

PULMONARY ARTERIES
AND VEINS

PULMONARY
ARTERY

SUPERIOR
VENA CAVA

SUPERIOR
VENA CAVA

AORTA

PULMONARY
VEIN

INFERIOR
VENA CAVA

RIGHT
ATRIUM

BRACHIAL
ARTERIES
AND VEINS

LEFT
ATRIUM

LEFT
VENTRICLE

FEMORAL
ARTERY

INFERIOR
VENA CAVA

RENAL
ARTERIES
AND VEINS

RIGHT
VENTRICLE

SEPTUM

GREAT
SAPHENOUS
VEIN

TRICUSPID
VALVE

ILIAC ARTERY
AND VEIN

When you listen to the heart with a
stethoscope, you can hear a "lub-dub"
sound. This is the sound the heart valves
make when snapping closed.

ACTIVITY: COLOR THE HEART

Heart diagrams are always shown from the patient's point of view, as if the patient was looking at the heart inside of their own chest. The right atrium is the patient's right side, not your right side. Color the heart according to the key shown. See page 68 for help.

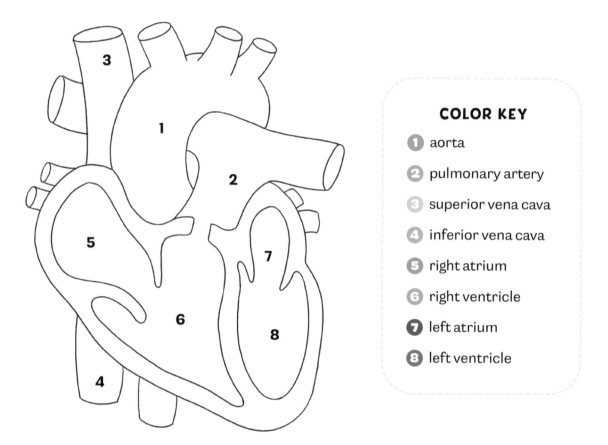

COLOR KEY

1 aorta
2 pulmonary artery
3 superior vena cava
4 inferior vena cava
5 right atrium
6 right ventricle
7 left atrium
8 left ventricle

➡ **Try This at Home**

As your blood is pumped through your arteries, you can feel it as a pulse. **Pulse rate** is measured in beats per minute (bpm). Let's find out what your pulse is! Locate your pulse in your wrist or neck and count how many beats you feel in one minute. Now do 30 jumping jacks. Check your pulse again. What happened to it?

ACTIVITY: DO YOU KNOW YOUR HEART?

Use the words below to fill in the blanks for each statement.

aorta	heart	capillaries
vena cava	blood	veins
double-loop cycle	red	oxygen

1. The circulatory system delivers _____ and nutrients

   to the body.

2. The main organ of the circulatory system is the _____,

   which pumps _____.

3. The vessels of your body may look blue under your skin, but the blood

   inside is _____.

4. Blood leaves the heart by traveling through a large artery called

   the _____.

5. Blood travels through _____ to return to the heart.

6. The largest vein in the body is the _____.

7. Small vessels called _____ deliver blood to body tissues.

8. The way blood travels through the heart is called a _____,

   because blood passes through the heart twice before going to the rest of the body.

Answers on page 68.

BREATHE IN, BREATHE OUT

All the cells in your body need oxygen to make energy for basic activities. You learned that the mitochondria are the "powerhouses" of the cell. These little organelles can work only when they have a constant supply of oxygen. The **respiratory system**'s job is to take oxygen from the air and deliver it to tissues while removing carbon dioxide, a waste product.

You hiccup when your diaphragm has a muscle spasm. The world record for the longest amount of time a person had the hiccups is 68 years.

DID YOU KNOW?

The **diaphragm** is a muscle under your ribs that contracts to help you breathe. When you breathe in, air passes down your throat and through a space called the **pharynx**. It then moves through the **larynx**, or the voice box. After that, it travels through a long tube called the **trachea**, or windpipe, and eventually to your two **lungs**.

The trachea splits into smaller tubes called **bronchi**. One bronchus goes to the left lung and one goes to the right lung. Like branches of a tree, the bronchi split into many smaller tubes called **bronchioles**. They are connected to air sacs called **alveoli**. The alveoli are covered in capillaries. These tiny sacs are where blood picks up oxygen and where it drops off carbon dioxide.

Your lungs have 1,500 miles of airways. That's about the distance from Boston, Massachusetts, to Miami, Florida!

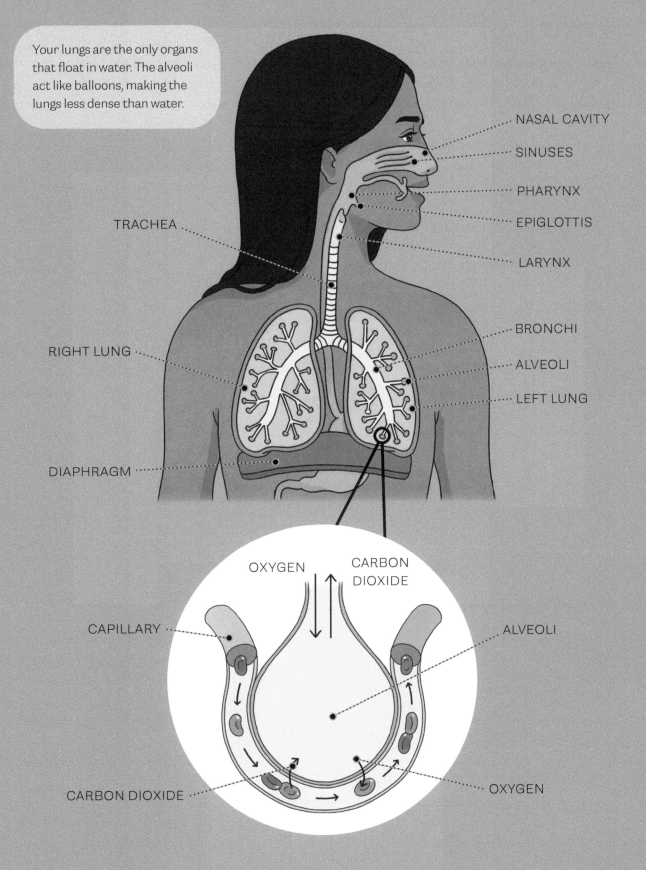

Your lungs are the only organs that float in water. The alveoli act like balloons, making the lungs less dense than water.

NASAL CAVITY

SINUSES

PHARYNX

EPIGLOTTIS

LARYNX

TRACHEA

BRONCHI

ALVEOLI

LEFT LUNG

RIGHT LUNG

DIAPHRAGM

OXYGEN

CARBON DIOXIDE

CAPILLARY

ALVEOLI

CARBON DIOXIDE

OXYGEN

ACTIVITY: ALL MIXED UP

Use the clues to unscramble the words. Each word answer has a number under a letter. Write the letter from that dash in the space with the same number for the riddle answer that follows. What's the answer to the riddle? See page 68 for help.

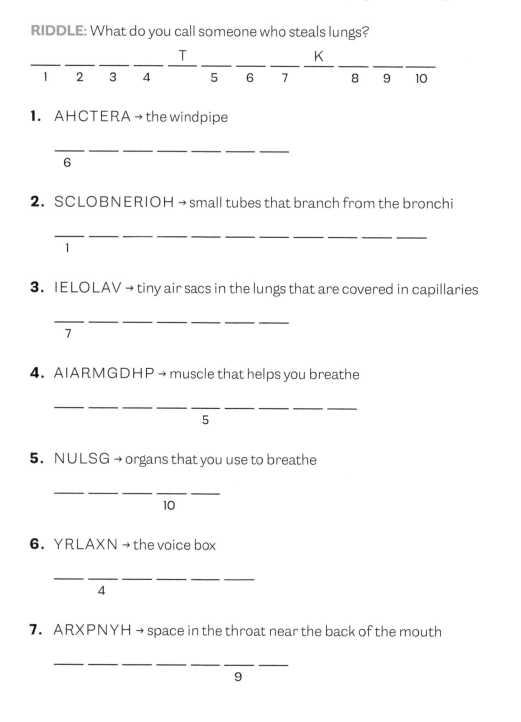

RIDDLE: What do you call someone who steals lungs?

___ ___ ___ ___ T ___ ___ ___ K ___ ___ ___
  1   2   3   4   5   6   7   8   9   10

1. AHCTERA → the windpipe

___ ___ ___ ___ ___ ___ ___
    6

2. SCLOBNERIOH → small tubes that branch from the bronchi

___ ___ ___ ___ ___ ___ ___ ___ ___ ___ ___
    1

3. IELOLAV → tiny air sacs in the lungs that are covered in capillaries

___ ___ ___ ___ ___ ___ ___
    7

4. AIARMGDHP → muscle that helps you breathe

___ ___ ___ ___ ___ ___ ___ ___ ___
                5

5. NULSG → organs that you use to breathe

___ ___ ___ ___ ___
            10

6. YRLAXN → the voice box

___ ___ ___ ___ ___ ___
        4

7. ARXPNYH → space in the throat near the back of the mouth

___ ___ ___ ___ ___ ___ ___
                9

8. HBNICOR → tubes that connect the trachea to the lungs

___ ___ ___ ___ ___ ___ ___
     2   8

9. GNOYXE → gas that moves from the air into the blood

___ ___ ___ ___ ___ ___
           3

ACTIVITY: BREATHING, STEP-BY-STEP

Number the diagram with the steps involved in breathing. See page 68 for help.

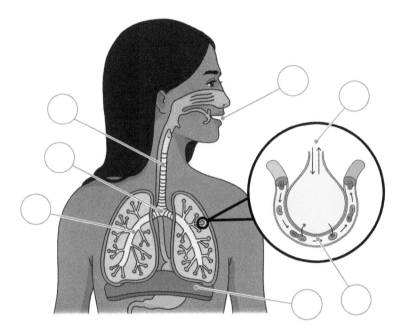

1. Diaphragm lowers and the chest expands

2. Air enters the mouth and nose

3. Air travels down the trachea

4. Air splits into the left and right bronchi

5. Air enters the bronchioles

6. Air enters the alveoli

7. Oxygen moves out of the air and into the bloodstream

> **➡ Try This at Home**
>
> **Lung capacity** is how much air your lungs can hold. If you take a deep breath and then force out as much air as you can, the amount of air you breathe out is your **vital capacity**. Let's measure it! Take the deepest breath you can and—using only one long breath—blow into the balloon. Ask someone bigger than you to do the same with a balloon the same size. Who has greater vital capacity?

MAKING SENSE
OF THE WORLD

Your brain is constantly gathering information about the world to respond to different situations. It uses **sense organs** like your skin, eyes, ears, nose, and mouth to detect changes in the environment. For example, if you smell smoke, your brain would tell you a fire is nearby and you should probably leave the area.

Motion sickness can happen when the fluid in the inner ear detects movement but the eyes don't, like when you are reading a book in a moving car. If you feel carsick, look out the window and focus on distant objects to help your brain make sense of the signals it is receiving from your ear.

DID YOU KNOW?

Each sense organ has thousands of **sensory receptors** that are specific for the jobs they do.

- Receptors in your skin detect heat and pressure.

- The rods and cones in your eyes detect light and different colors.

- Tiny cells in your ears sense vibrations to help you hear. Your ears also have fluid-filled chambers that help you balance.

- Your muscles even have **proprioceptive sensors** that let you know where your body parts are at all times. This is why you can touch your nose with your finger even with your eyes closed!

When your foot "falls asleep," the nerves that connect your foot to your brain have temporarily stopped working because pressure was applied for too long. The tingly sensation you feel are the nerves waking up.

Some people can "taste" colors or "see" music. This is because their brains process the sensory signals differently than everyone else.

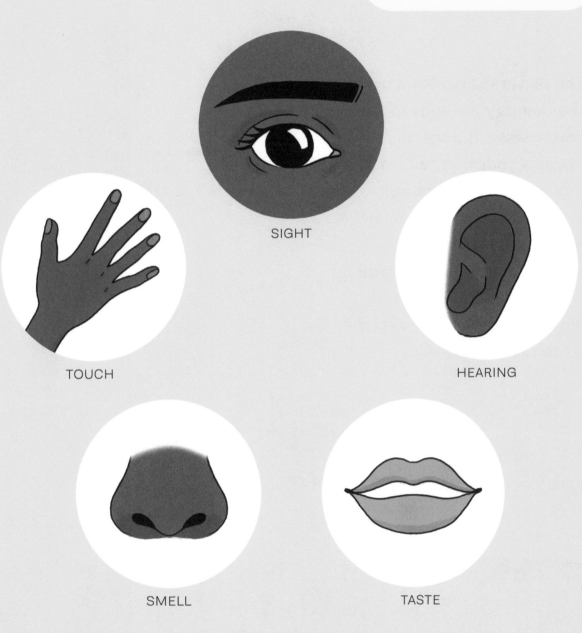

SIGHT

TOUCH

HEARING

SMELL

TASTE

SKIN, HAIR, AND NAILS

The skin in an important organ that keeps your body in homeostasis. It does this by keeping your body warm and moist inside, protecting it from bacteria, and providing information about the environment—like if something is hot or cold. Your hair and fingernails grow from special structures in your skin.

A substance in your skin called **melanin** gives it color and protects you from the sun's damaging rays. The more melanin you have, the darker your skin.

Your skin is constantly shedding old skin and replacing it with new skin. People shed about 40,000 skin cells every hour!

Your skin is the largest organ of the body and can weigh up to 8 pounds in adults. If you stretched it out, the skin would take up 22 square feet of space.

➡ Try This at Home

Unbend a paper clip to create two points about an inch apart. Gently place the two tips against different areas of your skin—like the back of your arm, your forehead, or your finger. If you feel two points, that means there are more receptors in that area. Which areas can you detect two points and which can detect only one point?

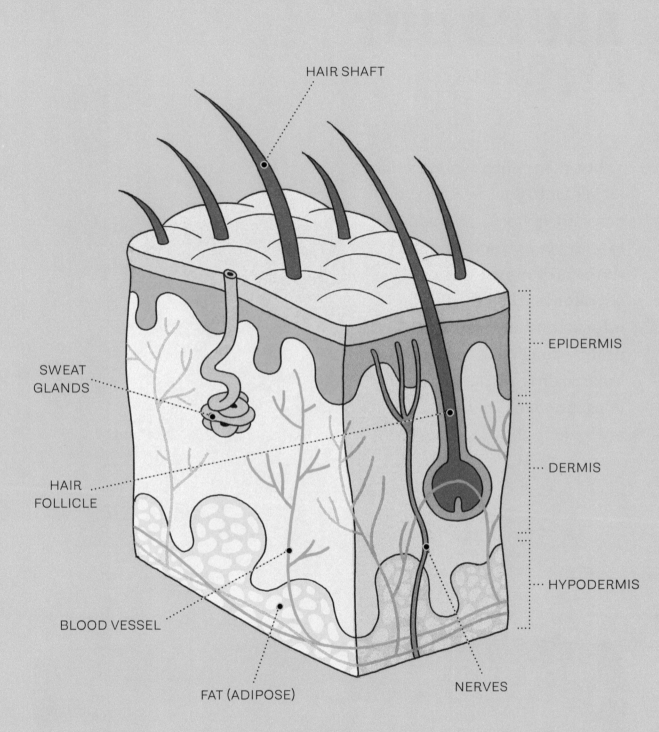

HAIR SHAFT

EPIDERMIS

SWEAT
GLANDS

DERMIS

HAIR
FOLLICLE

HYPODERMIS

BLOOD VESSEL

FAT (ADIPOSE)

NERVES

ALL ABOUT EYES

Your eyes are like windows that let light into your brain so you can see the world. The clear **lens** in your eye projects images onto the cells of the **retina** at the back of your eye. The retina takes this information and sends it to your brain through your **optic nerve**. Your brain translates those images and tells you whether you are looking at a bird or a plane.

The colored part of your eye is the **iris**. Some people have two different-colored irises—this is called **heterochromia**.

You have a blind spot in your vision where you can't see. This is where the optic nerve exits your eye, so there are no light receptors. You don't notice the blind spot because your brain fills in the gap.

Pink eye is caused by an infection in the **conjunctiva**, a thin skin that lines the inside of the eyelid. Conjunctivitis makes your eyes red and itchy, and it's very contagious!

➡ Try This at Home

Depth perception is the ability to tell how near or far away objects are. Hold a pencil in each hand with your arms stretched out. Try to touch the erasers together with both eyes open. Now close one eye and try it again. Were you able to connect the pencils both times?

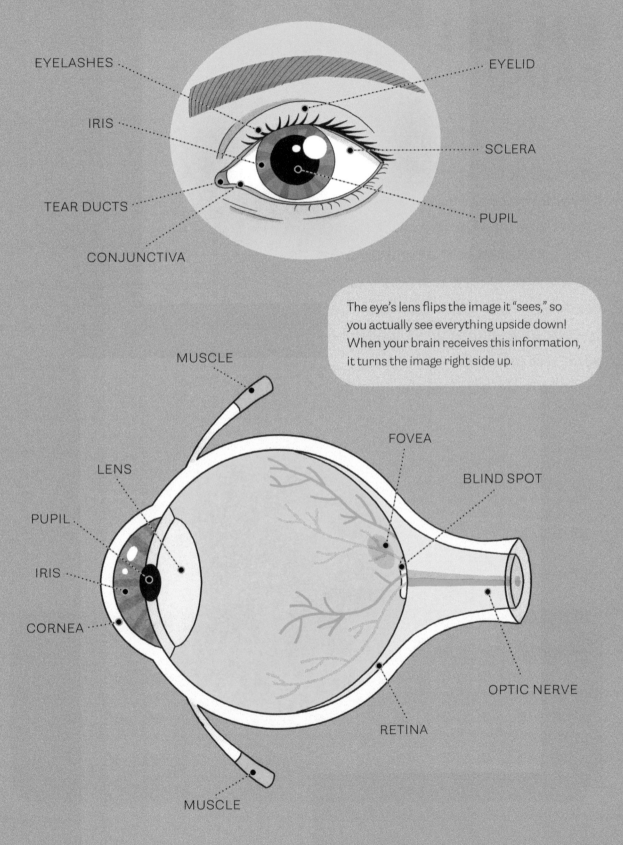

EYELASHES

EYELID

IRIS

SCLERA

TEAR DUCTS

PUPIL

CONJUNCTIVA

The eye's lens flips the image it "sees," so you actually see everything upside down! When your brain receives this information, it turns the image right side up.

MUSCLE

FOVEA

LENS

BLIND SPOT

PUPIL

IRIS

CORNEA

OPTIC NERVE

RETINA

MUSCLE

MAKING SENSE OF THE WORLD

I'M ALL EARS!

Your ear acts like a funnel to collect sound and send its vibrations into the ear canal. They go straight to the **tympanic membrane**—your eardrum. Your eardrum sends these vibrations to your inner ear, where receptors send the information to your brain to make sense of the sound.

Tiny glands in your ear produce **cerumen**, or earwax, which protects the ear by trapping dust and other particles. It might be gross, but it's important!

Receptors in your ear are called **hair cells**. They have little hairlike extensions of the cell membrane. Loud noises can damage these cells and lead to hearing loss. This is why you shouldn't listen to very loud music.

Your middle ear is connected to your throat by the **Eustachian tube**. If bacteria get stuck in the middle ear, that tube can swell shut, which can lead to **otitis**—an ear infection.

➡ Try This at Home

Sound can have a low pitch (like a rumble) or a high pitch (like a whistle). Receptors in the cochlea bend when sound vibrations hit them. This allows people to hear different volumes and pitches. Make an instrument using glasses and water! Fill glasses with different amounts of water. Then tap each with a spoon and listen to the sounds. Organize your glasses from low to high pitch. Can you play a simple tune?

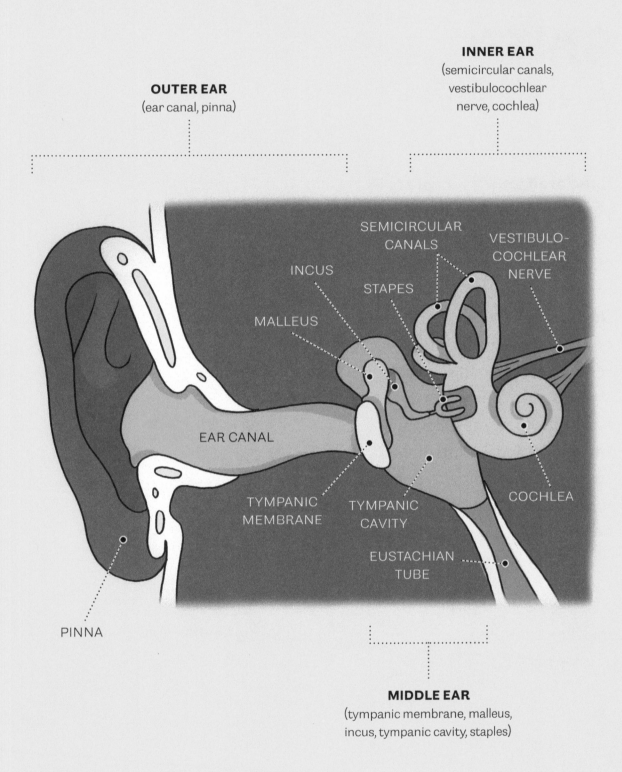

OUTER EAR
(ear canal, pinna)

INNER EAR
(semicircular canals,
vestibulocochlear
nerve, cochlea)

SEMICIRCULAR
CANALS

VESTIBULO-
COCHLEAR
NERVE

INCUS

STAPES

MALLEUS

EAR CANAL

COCHLEA

TYMPANIC
MEMBRANE

TYMPANIC
CAVITY

EUSTACHIAN
TUBE

PINNA

MIDDLE EAR
(tympanic membrane, malleus,
incus, tympanic cavity, staples)

SNIFF AND SMELL

Special **olfactory receptors** in your nose can detect chemicals in the air. When you inhale air, chemicals attach to different receptors that send information to your brain. You smell different odors depending on which receptors are sending signals. Your sense of smell can let you know if something is rotten or safe to eat and is even important for your sense of taste. Being able to smell your food makes it taste better or worse.

Boogers are formed when dust particles get trapped in the mucus in your nasal cavity. Small hairs called cilia wave together to sweep the mucus toward the nostrils.

When you sneeze, air, saliva, and mucus shoot out of your mouth and nose at up to 100 miles per hour!

Your sense of smell is connected to a part of the brain that processes memories and emotions. When you smell something familiar, it often brings back memories and emotions.

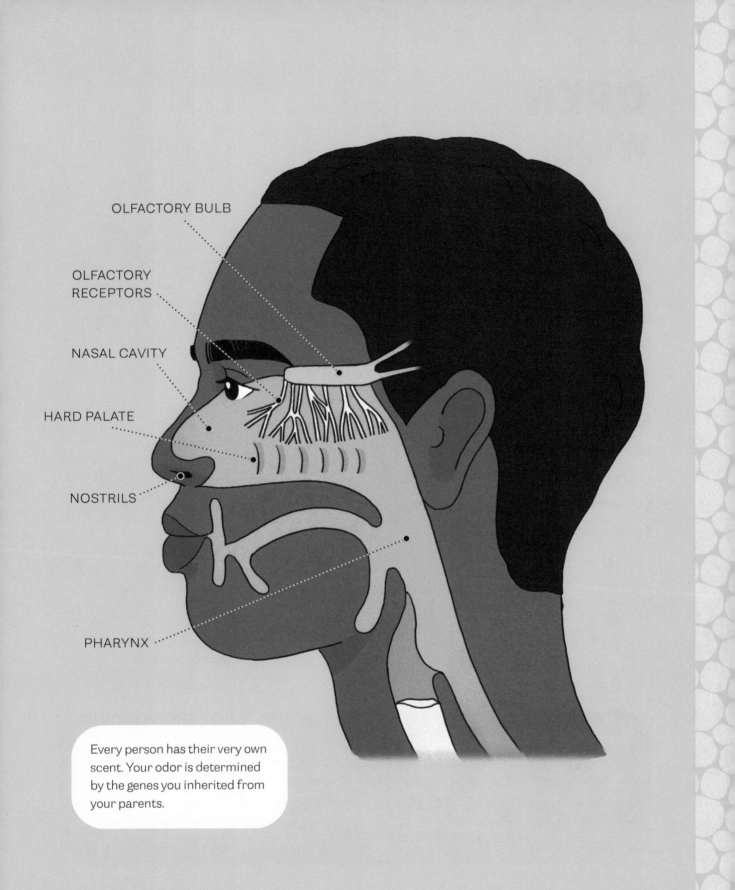

OLFACTORY BULB

OLFACTORY RECEPTORS

NASAL CAVITY

HARD PALATE

NOSTRILS

PHARYNX

Every person has their very own scent. Your odor is determined by the genes you inherited from your parents.

OPEN WIDE!

Your mouth is used for breathing, eating, and speaking. Human teeth are shaped for cutting and grinding food into smaller pieces. Your tongue, which is a very strong muscle for its size, moves food around your mouth, helps you speak, and is covered in receptors to help you taste different flavors. **Saliva** keeps your mouth moist and helps make food easy to swallow.

You were born without teeth. Your first set, or primary teeth, developed when you were 1 to 2 years old. When you were around 6 to 7 years old, your primary teeth started to be replaced by your secondary, or permanent teeth.

You have thousands of taste buds, but only five main taste types: sweet, sour, salty, bitter, and savory. These work together to give food unique tastes.

Saliva contains a chemical that breaks down starch into sugar. This is why you can leave a cracker on your tongue and it will dissolve even if you don't chew it. You might even notice the cracker starts to taste sweet.

➡ Try This at Home

Savory, also called **umami**, is a flavor that makes bacon and soy sauce so tasty. This flavor comes from an **amino acid** in food called **glutamate**. Locate something savory in your kitchen. Can you find examples of the other tastes, too? Write down examples from your kitchen for each flavor: sweet, sour, salty, bitter, and savory.

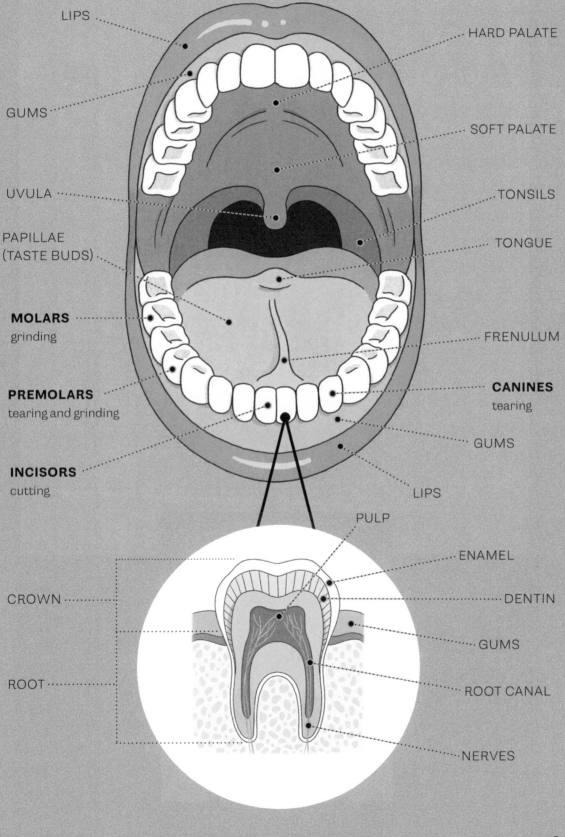

LIPS

HARD PALATE

GUMS

SOFT PALATE

UVULA

TONSILS

PAPILLAE
(TASTE BUDS)

TONGUE

MOLARS
grinding

FRENULUM

PREMOLARS
tearing and grinding

CANINES
tearing

GUMS

INCISORS
cutting

LIPS

PULP

ENAMEL

CROWN

DENTIN

GUMS

ROOT

ROOT CANAL

NERVES

YOUR BODY'S COMMUNICATION SYSTEM

Your **nervous system** works like an electrical network, where the wires are bundles of long cells called **neurons**. Neurons receive signals from other neurons in the body or the brain. They pass along the information to neurons nearby using electrical impulses and chemicals. For example, when you want to pick up something, your brain sends signals to your finger muscles to carry out the command.

The **autonomic nervous system** controls basic functions that you don't need to think about—like breathing, heart rate, and even digestion. This system is awake even when you are asleep!

When you dream, a brain chemical paralyzes your muscles, so you don't sleepwalk or move around. Imagine how dangerous it would be if you acted out your dreams!

DID YOU KNOW?

Your nervous system has two parts:

➡ The **central nervous system (CNS)** is made up of the brain and spinal cord. It helps manage all of your body's activities.

➡ The **peripheral nervous system (PNS)** contains all the nerves that connect the CNS to different parts of the body to control your muscles and senses. The PNS also controls your involuntary activities, like heart rate and digestion.

When a neuron gets a signal, it interacts with other neurons in the central nervous system. Often, the signal goes to the brain, which then decides how to react. The brain sends a message to different neurons that carry it to the part of the body that needs to react.

Reflexes are different. They are automatic responses to things that you don't need to think about—like when you touch something hot. Reflexes happen quickly because the signal just needs to go to the **spinal cord**, and not all the way to the brain.

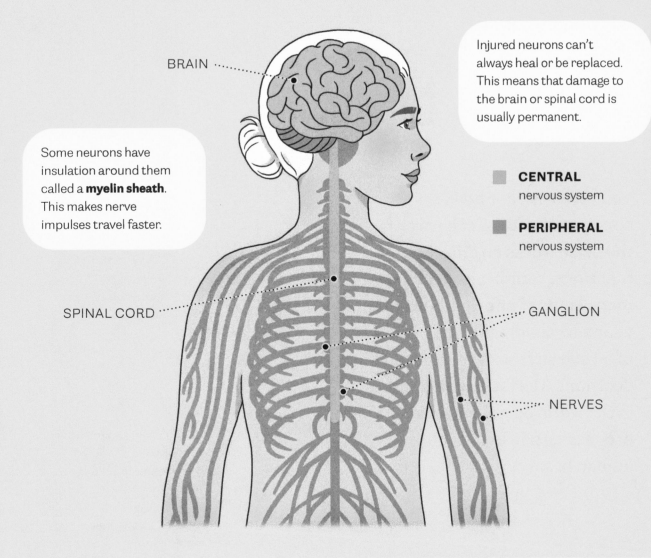

BRAIN

Injured neurons can't always heal or be replaced. This means that damage to the brain or spinal cord is usually permanent.

Some neurons have insulation around them called a **myelin sheath**. This makes nerve impulses travel faster.

CENTRAL
nervous system

PERIPHERAL
nervous system

SPINAL CORD

GANGLION

NERVES

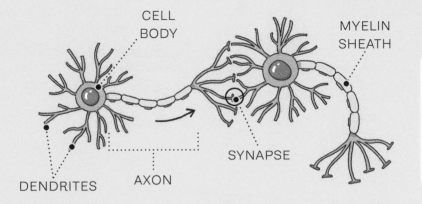

CELL BODY

MYELIN SHEATH

There is a gap between each neuron called a **synapse**. Chemicals called **neurotransmitters** cross these gaps and signal the next neuron. Many of these neurotransmitters also influence your moods!

SYNAPSE

DENDRITES

AXON

YOUR AMAZING BRAIN

Your brain is your body's command center. Each part of the brain works on different functions. Your brain can take in many kinds of information about your surroundings in the blink of an eye and make split-second decisions. The fastest computers in the world do not have the processing power of the human brain.

All brains have wrinkles on them called **gyri**. Every human brain has the same wrinkles. Doctors even use them as a sort of road map during brain surgery.

Inside your skull, your brain is filled with and surrounded by a liquid called **cerebrospinal fluid**. If you get hit in the head, your brain can slosh around and hit the inside of the skull. This can give you a **concussion**—a serious brain injury.

The brain can receive pain signals from other parts of the body, but the brain itself cannot feel pain. This is why surgeons can perform brain surgery while the patient is awake!

When you learn new things, your brain doesn't get larger in size. Instead, neurons increase the number of connections they have with other neurons.

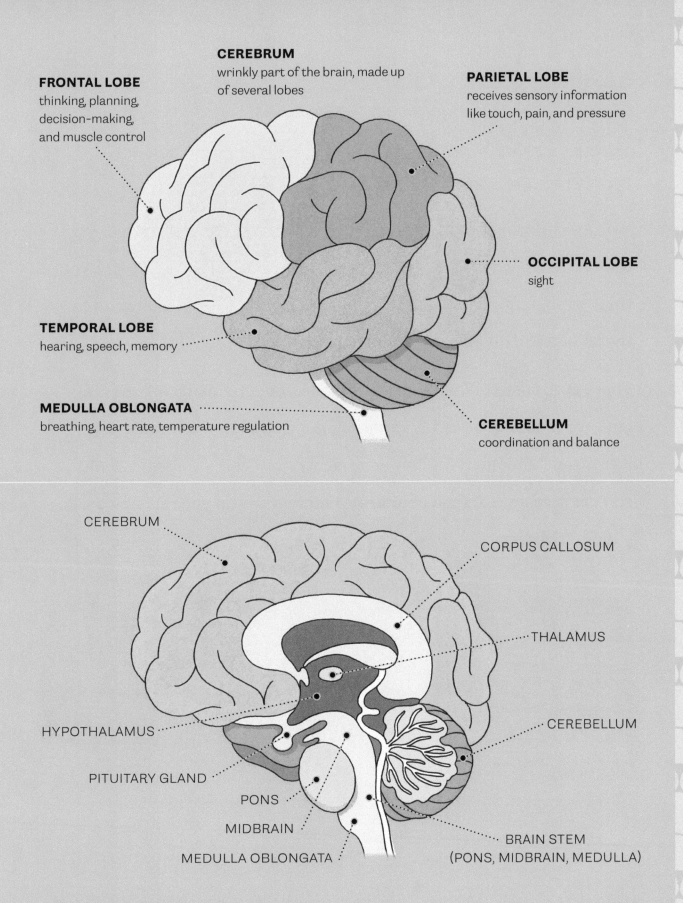

CEREBRUM
wrinkly part of the brain, made up of several lobes

FRONTAL LOBE
thinking, planning, decision-making, and muscle control

PARIETAL LOBE
receives sensory information like touch, pain, and pressure

OCCIPITAL LOBE
sight

TEMPORAL LOBE
hearing, speech, memory

MEDULLA OBLONGATA
breathing, heart rate, temperature regulation

CEREBELLUM
coordination and balance

CEREBRUM

CORPUS CALLOSUM

THALAMUS

HYPOTHALAMUS

CEREBELLUM

PITUITARY GLAND

PONS

MIDBRAIN

MEDULLA OBLONGATA

BRAIN STEM
(PONS, MIDBRAIN, MEDULLA)

ACTIVITY: PNS OR CNS?

Read the following story about a night in a haunted house. As you read, decide which of the activities stimulate the central nervous system (C), the peripheral nervous system (P), or both (B). Write your answers on the lines given. See page 69 for help.

Hint: It's "both" when an action involves moving or sensing (P) and thinking (C).

You are sitting on your bed planning what to wear on a school trip tomorrow ___ when you hear a strange noise from the hallway ___. You think to yourself, *What could that be? Is it a ghost?* ___ You duck under the covers and quietly ask, "Who's there?" ___

There is no answer. Your heart rate increases ___. You summon your courage to get out of bed ___ and slowly creep to the door and open it ___. You feel something soft and warm brush past your leg ___. You start to scream, but then your brain catches up and you realize it's just your cat, Mittens ___.

> ### ➡ Try This at Home
>
> Your brain can make sense of different messages at the same time, but when the messages don't match, your brain slows down. In the box below you'll see six colored words. Going from left to right, say the COLORS of the words as fast as you can. Now try just reading the words. Is it faster to say the colors or read the words?
>
> **Purple**   **Red**   **Yellow**   **Blue**   **Orange**   **Green**

ACTIVITY: USE YOUR BRAIN!

Draw a line to match each part of the brain to its job.

Frontal Lobe •   • receives sensory information

Parietal Lobe •   • hearing and speech

Temporal Lobe •   • decision-making

Occipital Lobe •   • sense of balance

Medulla Oblongata •   • heart and breathing rate

Cerebellum •   • sight

Answers on page 69.

LET'S EAT!

When you eat an apple, you are giving your body the energy and nutrients it needs to function. Your digestive system's job is to break down the apple to get nutrients like sugars and vitamins that your body can use.

A layer of mucus protects your stomach from being digested by its own acid. A person can get a painful sore called an **ulcer** if the acid gets through this mucus and damages the stomach.

The large intestine is a bigger "tube" than the small intestine, but the small intestine is much longer. It can stretch to 20 feet, which is much longer than you are tall!

DID YOU KNOW?

Digestion begins before you even swallow. Teeth grind the food and saliva breaks it down into simpler forms. When you swallow, the food travels down a tube called the **esophagus** and into the **stomach**. Acid in the stomach turns the food into a gooey substance called **chyme**. When chyme leaves the stomach, it enters the **small intestine**, where hairlike structures called **microvilli** absorb nutrients into the bloodstream.

Undigested food moves from the small intestine into the **large intestine**. Its main job is to absorb water and store undigested food. When you go to the bathroom, the remains of your meal are pushed out through the **anus** as feces (poop!).

The main path that food takes is the **alimentary canal**, but other organs help with digestion. For example, the **pancreas** makes chemicals called **enzymes** that break down sugars and proteins. The **liver**, the largest organ of this system, makes **bile** to help break down fat. Bile is stored in a pouch under the liver called the **gallbladder**.

ACTIVITY: QUIZ YOURSELF!

Color in the correct circle to indicate which statements are true and which are false. See page 69 for help.

1. Digestion begins in the stomach. (T) (F)

2. Food leaves the stomach and enters the small intestine. (T) (F)

3. Food travels through the liver on the way to the large intestine. (T) (F)

4. The liver is the largest organ of the digestive system. (T) (F)

5. The organ that absorbs nutrients into the blood is the large intestine. (T) (F)

6. Undigested food leaves the body through the pancreas. (T) (F)

7. Food leaves the stomach as a substance called chyme. (T) (F)

8. The gallbladder stores bile made by the liver. (T) (F)

9. The appendix is attached to the liver. (T) (F)

10. Undigested food, or waste, is stored in the rectum. (T) (F)

> ➡ **Try This at Home**
>
> Food moves through the alimentary canal because of muscular contractions called **peristalsis**. Try making an esophagus to see how this works. Cut off the toe end of a small tube sock (with your parents' permission). This is your esophagus. Now put a plastic egg or ball into the sock and try to push it out the other end. This is how muscles work to push food through!

WASTE
BE GONE!

Your two **kidneys** are amazing filters. They remove waste from the blood and turn it into urine. Urine travels out of the kidneys and down tubes called **ureters**. Urine eventually ends up in the **urinary bladder**. Your bladder is waterproof and stretchy. Eventually, it gets full enough that you notice that you need to urinate (pee)!

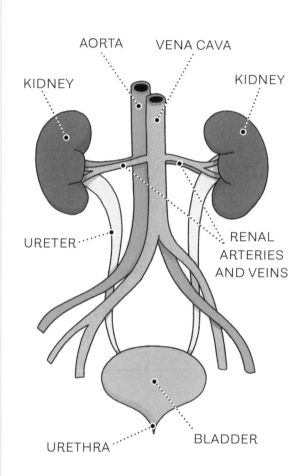

AORTA   VENA CAVA

KIDNEY   KIDNEY

URETER

RENAL ARTERIES AND VEINS

URETHRA   BLADDER

Urine exits the body through a tube called the **urethra**.

A chemical in urine called **urea** gives it that familiar smell. Urea turns into **ammonia**, which is a common cleaning product. Before there was detergent, urine was used to clean clothes!

Urine is mostly made of water and is usually yellow in color. Darker urine can mean you have an infection or need to drink more water. Some medications and food dye can turn your pee green!

ACTIVITY: WORD SEARCH

The words below are hidden in this word search. Circle the words as you find them.

WORD BANK

bladder	ureter	urine	blood
kidney	urethra	urea	waste

```
E   U   R   E   T   E   R   F   B   E
U   C   C   X   L   A   F   O   K   E
R   Z   B   U   R   E   T   H   R   A
E   W   X   L   P   K   M   K   B   C
A   K   A   R   A   I   F   U   L   U
F   Y   K   S   M   D   R   J   O   R
K   B   T   B   T   N   D   D   O   I
J   J   P   T   S   E   G   E   D   N
F   R   N   H   O   Y   Y   V   R   E
O   G   K   C   O   A   R   R   T   V
```

Answers on page 69.

GETTING RID OF GERMS

Remember the last time you were sick? You probably had a runny nose, a cough, and maybe even a fever. While these symptoms are not fun, they are important because they mean that your **immune system** is fighting to get rid of the germs making you sick. Some illnesses are caused by tiny microbes called **pathogens**. Pathogens can be bacteria, viruses, or fungi.

When you are sick, a doctor feels your throat to see if the lymph nodes are swollen, which indicates you are fighting an infection.

DID YOU KNOW?

Your body has defenses to prevent pathogens from getting in. Your skin keeps bacteria or viruses from entering the body, and sticky mucus in the nasal cavity traps germs. These protections are part of your **innate immunity**—your body's first line of defense.

When your innate defenses fail, **adaptive immunity** kicks in. If a cold virus gets into your respiratory system, your **white blood cells** produce **antibodies**. These antibodies latch on to the invaders and mark them so that other immune cells can find and destroy them. **Macrophages** are cells that surround and gobble up the invaders. Other white blood cells trigger apoptosis in any marked cells. The **phlegm** you cough up is the remains of your immune cells and the germs they were fighting.

The **spleen** is an organ that you can live without, but it does have a function in the immune system. Its job is to destroy worn-out red blood cells and kill pathogens in the bloodstream.

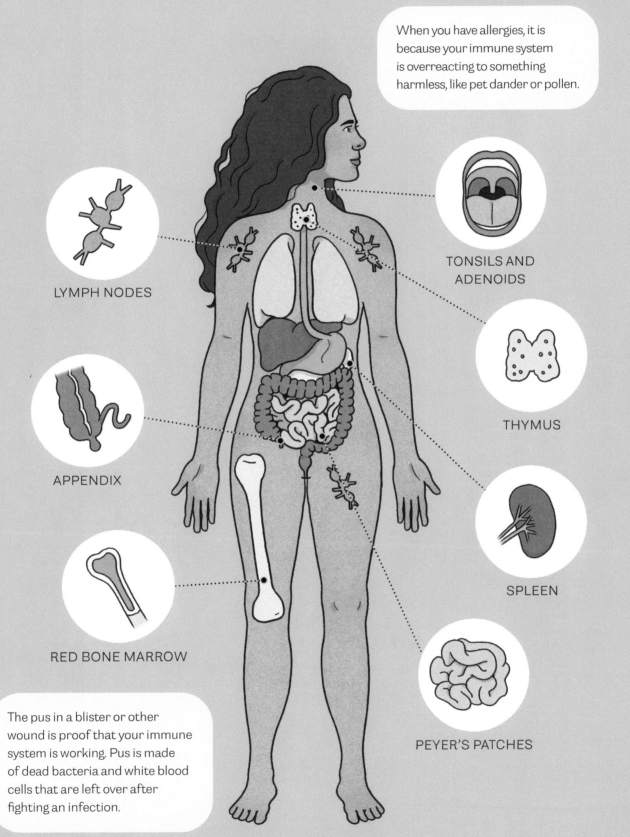

When you have allergies, it is because your immune system is overreacting to something harmless, like pet dander or pollen.

TONSILS AND ADENOIDS

LYMPH NODES

THYMUS

APPENDIX

SPLEEN

RED BONE MARROW

The pus in a blister or other wound is proof that your immune system is working. Pus is made of dead bacteria and white blood cells that are left over after fighting an infection.

PEYER'S PATCHES

ACTIVITY: HOW DO VACCINES WORK?

Have you ever wondered how vaccines work to keep you healthy? Here's a diagram showing how vaccination protects us from diseases. Color the virus and B cells (a type of white blood cell) according to the key!

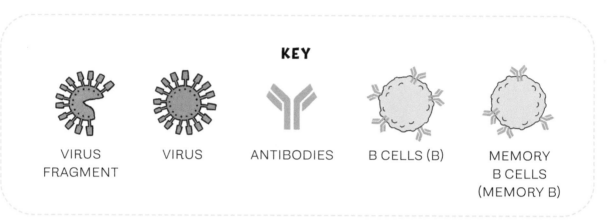

KEY

VIRUS FRAGMENT   VIRUS   ANTIBODIES   B CELLS (B)   MEMORY B CELLS (MEMORY B)

1. Weakened pathogen, like a virus fragment, is injected into your body.

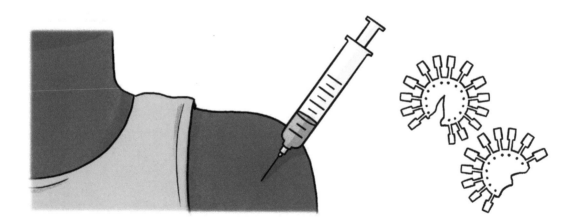

2. Your white blood cells produce memory B cells and antibodies to fight that specific virus.

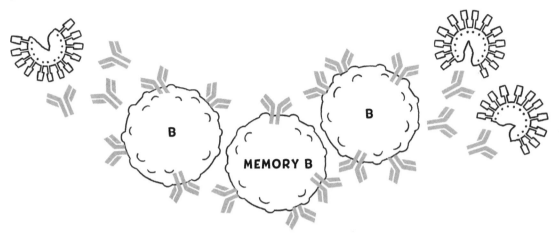

3. If the same virus shows up in your body later, now your memory B cells can recognize it more quickly and produce antibodies to fight it.

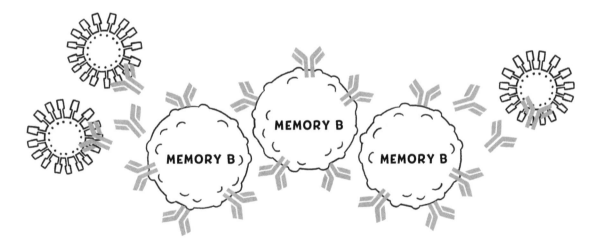

➡ Try This at Home

The average body temperature for humans is 98.6°F. Your typical temperature might be higher or lower than that, and it can change throughout the day. Use a thermometer to take your temperature over several days and keep track of the numbers. What is *your* average?

YOUR CHANGING BODY

As your body grows in size, it also changes to prepare for adulthood. Some of you may grow breasts and start your period. Others may become taller and grow facial hair. This process, called **puberty**, allows your body to make important sex cells. Puberty usually begins between ages 9 and 14, but it can start earlier or later. Everyone grows at their own pace!

When one fertilized egg splits into two different embryos, identical twins are the result. They each have the same genes and look almost exactly alike.

During puberty, hormones increase the activity of special sweat glands called **apocrine glands**. Some are located under your arms. When that sweat mixes with bacteria, it can make a bad smell, often called BO, or body odor.

DID YOU KNOW?

Sex cells allow humans to reproduce. In females, **egg cells** are made by the **ovaries**. After puberty, an egg is released once a month. The egg can be fertilized by a **sperm**, which is produced in the **testes** of males. If the egg is not fertilized, it will leave the body, along with the lining of the **uterus,** during **menstruation**. This happens about once a month.

When a sperm fertilizes an egg, an **embryo** forms. The embryo grows into a **fetus**, which can be born as a baby about nine months after fertilization.

Genes control traits and what you look like. Half of your genes came from the egg, and the other half from the sperm. This explains why people usually look like both of their parents. Each time a sperm and egg combine, different genes are taken from each. This is why brothers and sisters never look exactly alike.

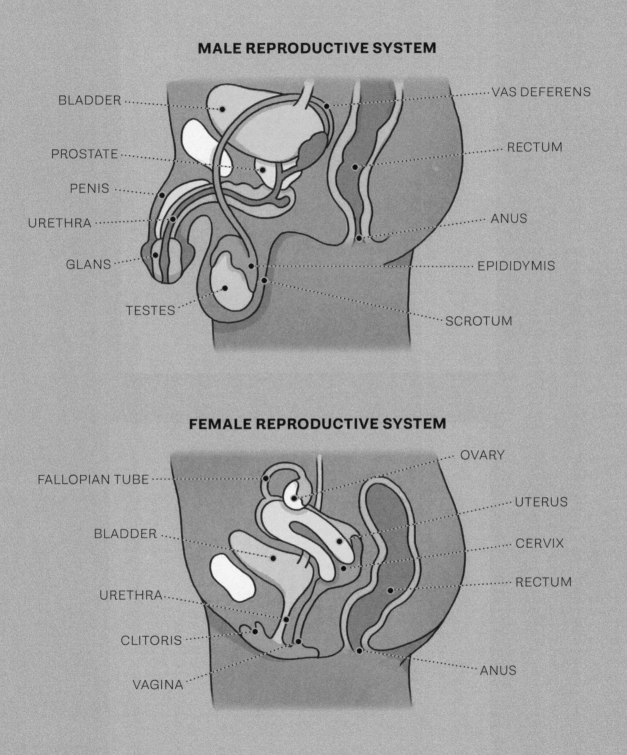

MALE REPRODUCTIVE SYSTEM

BLADDER

VAS DEFERENS

PROSTATE

RECTUM

PENIS

URETHRA

ANUS

GLANS

EPIDIDYMIS

TESTES

SCROTUM

FEMALE REPRODUCTIVE SYSTEM

OVARY

FALLOPIAN TUBE

UTERUS

BLADDER

CERVIX

RECTUM

URETHRA

CLITORIS

VAGINA

ANUS

ACTIVITY: WHOSE ANATOMY?

Complete the diagram by putting the organs usually found in assigned females in the correct circle, then do the same for assigned males. Some organs are found in both. Put those in the space in the center of the diagram.

WORD BANK

prostate	testes	rectum	vas deferens
vagina	urethra	fallopian tube	anus
uterus	bladder		

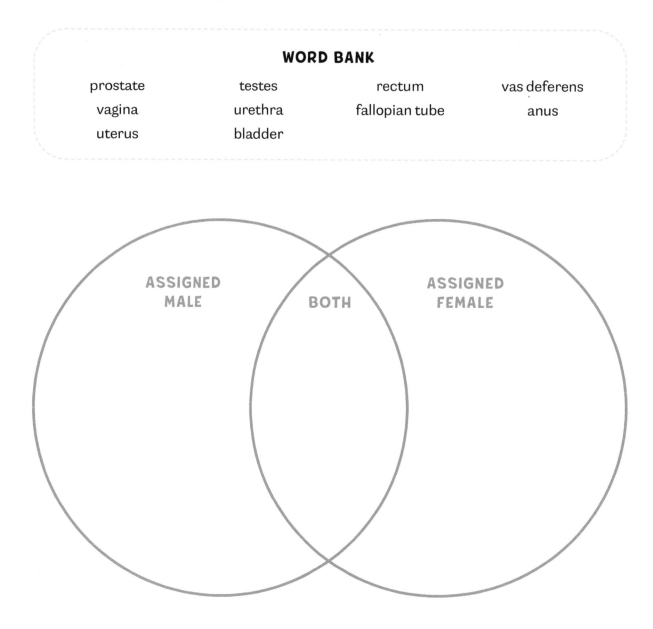

ASSIGNED MALE   BOTH   ASSIGNED FEMALE

Answers on page 69.

TAKING CARE
OF YOUR BODY

Your body works hard to help you thrive, but you also have to do your part to stay healthy.

➤ **Balanced Nutrition -** Vitamins and minerals in fruits and vegetables help you to grow strong bones and keep your nervous system's electrical signals firing.

➤ **Get Rested -** Your brain and immune system work best when you get enough sleep.

➤ **Stay Active -** Stretching and exercising help you grow muscles and can even improve circulation.

Taking care of your body means taking care of all of the systems!

The amount of sleep you need changes as you grow up. An 8-year-old needs 10 to 11 hours of sleep each night to be healthy.

Devices with screens give off a blue light, which can disrupt your sleep cycles. Limit your screen time, especially before bed!

When you play sports, you lose a lot of water. Coaches sometimes give players a drink that has extra minerals called **electrolytes**. These drinks replace water and salts lost through sweat and breathing.

➡ **Try This at Home**

One thing you can do to stay healthy is wash your hands regularly. Handwashing can protect you against germs, but you need to use soap and water and scrub for 20 seconds. That is about how long it takes to sing "Happy Birthday" twice. Try washing your hands and singing! What other songs are about 20 seconds long?

ANSWER KEY

FILL IN THE BLANKS (PAGE 12)

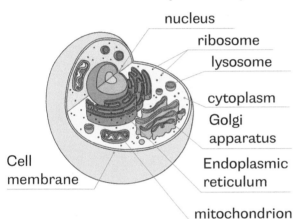

nucleus
ribosome
lysosome
cytoplasm
Golgi apparatus
Endoplasmic reticulum
mitochondrion
Cell membrane

NAME THE BONE! (PAGE 18)

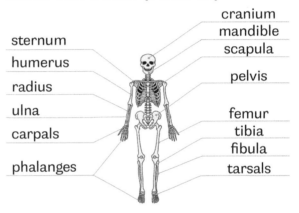

cranium
mandible
scapula
pelvis
femur
tibia
fibula
tarsals
sternum
humerus
radius
ulna
carpals
phalanges

HELP DR. MITO (PAGE 13)

Mitochondria
Lysosome
Nucleus
Cell membrane
Golgi apparatus
Ribosomes
Endoplasmic reticulum

CROSSWORD PUZZLE (PAGE 19)

Across
2. hinge
6. humerus
9. patella
10. carpals
12. mandible

Down
1. femur
3. tibia
4. vertebrae
5. phalanges
7. ulna
8. tarsals
11. ribs

MATCH THE MUSCLES (PAGE 22)

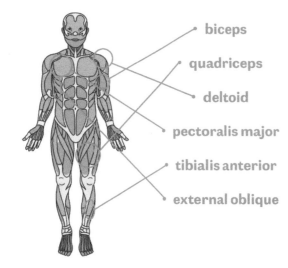

- biceps
- quadriceps
- deltoid
- pectoralis major
- tibialis anterior
- external oblique

DO YOU KNOW YOUR MUSCLES? (PAGE 23)

1. cardiac
2. biceps
3. gluteus maximus
4. myofibrils
5. heat
6. voluntary
7. involuntary
8. triceps
9. cardiac
10. involuntary

COLOR THE HEART (PAGE 26)

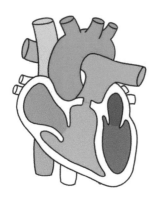

DO YOU KNOW YOUR HEART? (PAGE 27)

1. oxygen
2. heart, blood
3. red
4. aorta
5. veins
6. vena cava
7. capillaries
8. double-loop cycle

ALL MIXED UP (PAGE 30)

RIDDLE: breathtaking
1. trachea
2. bronchioles
3. alveoli
4. diaphragm
5. lungs
6. larynx
7. pharynx
8. bronchi
9. oxygen

BREATHING, STEP-BY-STEP (PAGE 31)

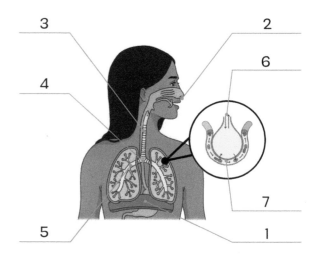

PNS OR CNS? (PAGE 48)

C
B
C
B
P
C
B
B
C

USE YOUR BRAIN! (PAGE 49)

Frontal Lobe • → receives sensory information

Parietal Lobe • → hearing and speech

Temporal Lobe • → decision-making

Occipital Lobe • → sense of balance

Medulla Oblongata • → heart and breathing rate

Cerebellum • → sight

NAME THAT ORGAN! (PAGE 54)

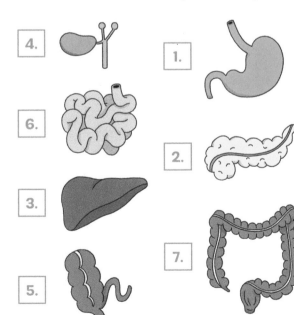

QUIZ YOURSELF! (PAGE 55)

1. F
2. T
3. F
4. T
5. F
6. F
7. T
8. T
9. F
10. T

WORD SEARCH (PAGE 57)

WHOSE ANATOMY? (PAGE 64)

Assigned Male: prostate, testes, vas deferens
Assigned Female: vagina, fallopian tube, uterus
Both: urethra, bladder, rectum, anus

RESOURCES

Books

First Human Body Encyclopedia by DK
A great introduction to the inner workings of the human body.

Human Body! by DK
A visual encyclopedia featuring computer generated 3D imagery of the body.

The Fantastic Body: What Makes You Tick & How You Get Sick by Howard Bennett
Written by a pediatrician, this book is stuffed with fun facts, diagrams, and gross stories.

Digital Resources

Get Body Smart
(GetBodySmart.com)
A fully animated and interactive e-book about human anatomy and physiology.

Innerbody
(Innerbody.com/htm/body.html)
This website includes details about the main body systems and allows children to explore both 2D and 3D models of the body.

Science Kids, Human Body for Kids
(ScienceKids.co.nz/humanbody.html)
This website features games, experiments, quizzes, images, and projects for learning about the human body.

Games and Models

Anatomy Models Bundle Set from Learning Resources
Includes small plastic models of the body, brain, heart, and skeleton for children to assemble.

Fascinating Facts Human Body Game by Lakeshore
Play a game while exploring the human body from the inside out with a 10.5-inch model and quiz cards.

INDEX

Sperm, 10, 11, 62
Sphygmomanometers, 24
Spinal cord, 44–45
Spleen, 58, 59
Spongy bone tissue, 14, 17
Stethoscopes, 25
Stomach, 50–51
Synapses, 45

T

Taste, 33, 42–43
Taste buds, 42–43
Teeth, 42–43
Temperature, 61
Temporal lobe, 47
Tendons, 14
Testes, 62
Thymus, 59
Tissues, 10
Tongue, 42–43
Tonsils, 59
Touch, 33, 34–35
Trachea, 28
Triceps, 20
Tympanic membrane, 38–39

U

Ulcers, 50
Urea, 56
Ureters, 56
Urethra, 56
Urinary system, 9
Urine, 56
Uterus, 62

V

Vaccines, 60–61
Veins, 25
Vena cava, 24, 25
Ventricles, 24, 25

Vital capacity, 31
Voluntary muscles, 20

W

Wadlow, Robert ("Alton
    Giant"), 8
White blood cells, 58, 60-61

Y

Yellow marrow, 14, 17

ABOUT THE AUTHOR

SHANNAN MUSKOPF, MS, studied biology and education at the University of Illinois, eventually obtaining an MS in teaching biology. She has taught biology, AP biology, and anatomy and physiology for more than 20 years at a public high school.

Shannan also developed the website BiologyCorner.com to share resources with students and with other teachers. The site focuses on learning activities for exploring biology and anatomy, as well as sharing videos and images of class projects.

ABOUT THE ILLUSTRATOR

CHRISTY NI developed a lifelong passion for the arts when she started her first side hustle tracing animals for her kindergarten classmates. As a budding artist, she went on to earn her BFA in illustration from the Maryland Institute College of Art. She is currently employed as a full-time illustrator for Hallmark in Kansas City, where her art can be seen on a variety of products ranging from pop-up greeting cards to Christmas ornaments.

CPSIA information can be obtained
at www.ICGtesting.com
Printed in the USA
JSHW052141261021
19878JS00004B/13